quick

18

and

easy

25

Article
Marketing

TABLE OF CONTENTS

ARTICLE MARKETING EXPLAINED

One way of promoting your website and product can be achieved for **FREE**. As an additional bonus, this "free" method can boost your sites and sales, doubling and even tripling your income.

Articles. One of the easiest ways to promote your website in order to generate traffic and increase your earnings.

How does this work?

Write articles relating to your website and submit them to "free content" submission sites. Easy to do, takes little time and can increase your website traffic, sales and of course, your income.

How can article writing boost traffic and income?

The article on the free content site contains a link to your own website. Readers, after reading your articles, may choose to click on the link and pay you an unexpected visit. Having them on the free content sites is also making these articles available to other webmasters who may wish to publish that article on their site.

If they do, your article will include a link back to your site. And anyone who reads the article on that site can still click on the link to visit your site.

As the list of your published articles grow larger, and more and more of them are appearing on different websites, the total number of links to your site increases also.

Major search engines are placing a lot of significance on incoming links to websites so they can determine the importance of a certain site.

The more incoming links the website has, the more importance search engines attaches to it. This will then increase your website's placement in the search results.

If you site is into promoting a product or service, the links that your articles have achieved will mean more potential customers for you. Even if visitors only browse through, you never know if they might be in need of what you are offering in the future.

There are also those who already have specific things they need on their mind but cannot decide yet between the many choices online. Chances are, they may stumble upon one of your articles, gets interested by the contents you wrote, go to your site and became enticed by your promotions.

See how easy that is?

Search engines do not just index the websites, they also index published articles.

They also index any article that is written about your own website's topic. So once someone searches for that same topic, the list of results will have your site or may even show the articles that you have written.

And to think, no effort on your part was used to bring them to your site. **Just your published articles and the search engines.**

It is no wonder why many webmasters are suddenly reviving their old writing styles and taking time to write more articles about their site than doing other means of promotion.

Getting their site known is easier if they have articles increasing their links and traffic and making it accessible for visitors searching the Internet. Since many people are now taking their buying needs online, having your site on the search engines through your articles is one way of letting them know about you and your business.

The good thing with articles is that you can write about things that people would want to know about. This can be achieved in the lightest mood but professional manner, with a little not-so-obvious sales pitch added.

If you think about it, only a few minutes of your time is spent on writing one article and submitting to free content site. In the shortest span of time also, those are distributed to more sites than you can think of. Even before you know what is happening, you are getting more visitors than you previously had.

If you think you are wasting your time writing these articles, fast forward to the time when you will see them printed and wide-spread on the Internet. Not to mention the sudden attention and interest that people are giving your website and your products or services.

Try writing some articles and you will be assured of the sudden surge in site traffic, link popularity and interest. Before you know it, you will be doubling and even tripling your earnings.

Nothing like getting benefits for something you got for free!

THE 4 THINGS ALL ARTICLES MUST HAVE

The importance of articles in today's websites and Internet based companies are immeasurable. They dictate a lot in the success and the drive of traffic into one's site. It has become a key element in making a site work and earns a profit. A website operator and owner must have the good sense to include articles in his or her site that will work for them and earn them the many benefits articles can give to their site.

Articles have been known to be the driving force in driving traffic to a website. Articles are a factor in giving site high rankings in search result pages. The higher a site ranks the bigger slice of the traffic flow pie he gets. With a huge number in traffic flow, there are more profits and more potential for other income generating schemes as well.

But, it is not just about stuffing your site with articles; they have certain requirements as well.

These requirements must be met to obtain the maximum benefits an article will provide for your site. A well written article will catch the eyes and interest of your customers and keep them coming back for more. They would also be able to recommend your site to others.

Here are some tips to help you and assist you in making your articles. Below you will read about four things all articles must have to make it successful and helpful in making your site a profit earning and traffic overflowing site.

Keywords and Keyword Phrases.

An article must always be centered on the keywords and keyword phrases. As each website visitor goes to a site, there are those who are just merely browsing but actually looking for a specific something. When this happens, a searcher usually goes to a search engine and types in the keywords they are looking for (e.g. Toyota Camry, Meningitis, Tax Lawyer etc.). It could be anything they want.

The Important thing is that you have an article that has the keywords that are related to your site.

For example, if you maintain an auto parts site, you must be able t have articles about cars and their parts. There are many tools in the Internet that provides service in helping a webmaster out in determining what keywords and keyword phrases are mostly sought out. You can use this tool to determine what keywords to use and write about.

Keyword Density

Know that you have your keywords and keyword phrases, you must use them fully. An article must have good keyword density for a search engine to "feel" its presence. Articles should at least have ten to fifteen percent of keyword density in their content for search engines to rank a site high in their search results. Getting a high rank is what articles do best for a site.

Keyword density is the number of times a keyword or keyword phrase is used on an article. The number varies depending on the number of words used in an article. An effective article must have a keyword density that is not too high or too low.

With a very high density, the essence of the article is lost and may turn off a reader as well as the search engines. It comes off as overeager. A low number may be ignored by the search engines.

Good Article Content

Like what is stated above, you cannot just riddle an article with keywords. They must also be regarded as good reading materials. Articles must be able to entertain people as well as provide good information and help for their needs.

Articles should be written well with correct spelling and good grammar. If you want people to trust you, make your work good and well thought out.

People respond well to figures, facts and statistics. Try to get great information and as many facts as you can. A good and well written article will boost your reputation as an expert in your chosen field or topic. As more people believe in you. They will be able to trust you and your products.

Linking Articles

And another important thing to remember: if you are going to submit articles to E-zines and/or contribute your articles to newsletters and other sites, DON'T ever forget to include a link to your site. A little resource box with a brief description of your site and you should always be placed right after your articles that you have submitted. If people like your articles, they will most likely click on the link directing them to your site.

HOW TO CREATE AN OUTLINE FOR ALL OF YOUR ARTICLE

We've done it through junior high, it expanded longer through high school. Then on college it became chapters. No matter how many times a person have done it, writing articles has proven to be a task many has continuously avoided. Now at a time when writing articles could help your job or work, facing the job at hand can be still faced with unfriendly behavior.

While there are a great number of people who do not have the same attitude in article writing as others, there are still those who would rather walk in piping hot coals than do some article writing. What set other people apart from other towards article writing is that they are prepared and has some methods and procedures in writing articles.

One of the methods you can use to prepare yourself when tasked to write in article is creating an outline first. Creating an outline for all your articles makes you prepared. You have an idea of what to do first and make a plan for your succeeding steps. Being prepared makes the job easier and faster. Being organized will allow for disorientation to be shunned away.

An outline can act as the design or blueprint for your article. This will guide you in creating the introduction, body and conclusion of your article.

Here in this point, you can write down some of the ideas and sentences that you feel will look good in your article. This could be some of the focal point that could help make your article creative, interesting and appealing to a reader.

A carefully planned and fully prepared project would guarantee and ensure a problem and worry free procedure that can virtually go without any hassles.

Creating an outline for all your articles will get you ready and breeze through writing an article in no time at all. Here I will provide you with some tips and guidelines in how to create an outline for all of your articles.

Do a couple of brainstorming and jot down your brilliant ideas first. Think of some ways to attract the interest of your reader. Designate a time frame where you can write down all the ideas that you can use for your articles.

By this time you should have done all your research and information searching. Review and reread your ideas and notes, gain mastery and sufficient familiarity with your topic so that writing them down later own would be easy for you.

The next step is to discover your sub topic and sub titles. As you would provide a first sentence for your article, one that would immediately grab the attention of your reader, you would need some as well for your sub topics.

To be concise, you would need to get all the facts that will support and go against your point. These are the frames or skeleton of your article, now its time to add the flesh and the meat of your article.

You will need to connect all your paragraphs and sub topics. This will form the body of your Article.

While the introduction will usher in the ideas of your paragraph, you will need a conclusion. The conclusion will wrap up your points and drive in what you are saying in your article.

The outline for your article would also require you to write a draft first. This may take more than one attempt but remember that it is called a draft for a reason.

Your outline shall be perfected as each draft is written and this draft is meant for *your eyes only* so there's no reason to feel ashamed.

As you go on, you will clearly see the bigger picture and write an article that will perfectly suit what is demanded of it.

Reread and reread what you have written down. Always refer to your outline so that you wont drift away from what you had first written down. Its not hard to be caught in the moment and get lost in your writing frenzy.

Your outline will help you keep in track. All those hours spent in outlining your article will not go to waste. This will serve as your guide in writing articles. Trust and rely on your outline because this will prove to be a very helpful tool in writing all of your articles.

5 EASY WAYS TO GET YOUR CREATIVE JUICES GOING

Writing an article doesn't just mean putting down thoughts into words then typing and writing it. You have to capture the interest of your readers and get them to keep on reading. To send your message across you have to get the attention of the reader and have a firm grasp of their interest and pique their curiosity.

The main ingredient in baking up an article is a large dose of creativity. While creativity may come natural to many people, some just gets into a block or something to that effect that can drive someone crazy. Many writers have literally torn their hair out when they get writers block and just can't seem to get their creative juices flowing.

Putting words into images in the readers mind is an art. A clear and crisp depiction requires a certain flair that only creativity can provide.

Similes and metaphors help a lot, but the way an article gets entwined word for word, sentence by sentence then paragraph by paragraph into a whole article develops the essence of the article.

So just what do you have to do when nothing comes to mind? There is no surefire ways to get the perfect ideas but there are easy ways to get your creative juices flowing. No one can guarantee you of having the perfect mindset but many methods may aid you in achieving that state of mind. Here are five easy ways for that.

1) Keep a diary or a journal with you always.

Ideas can be triggered by anything you may hear, see, or smell. Your senses are your radar in finding great ideas. Write all of them into a journal and keep it with you for future reference. You may also write down anything that you have read or heard, someone's ideas could be used to develop your own ideas and this is not stealing. Remember that ideas and creativity can come from anywhere; it's the development of the idea that makes it unique.

2) Relax and take time to sort things out.

A jumbled mind cannot create any space for new ideas. Everyone must have a clear mind if one wishes to have their creativity in full speed. Get rid of all obstacles that can be a hindrance to your creativity. If you are bothered by something, you cannot force your mind to stay focused.

Try to relax every time that you can and think about your experiences and interactions with others. Your experiences are what shape your mindset and your opinions which could be reflected on your writings. Try to discover yourself, find out what triggers your emotions. Discover what inspires you and what ticks you off. You can use these emotions to help you in expressing yourself and your ideas, with this you can grow creatively.

3) Create a working place that can inspire your creativeness.

Your working place can be quite a hindrance if it doesn't make you feel happy or relaxed.

Creativity comes from being in a good state of mind and a messed up workplace that causes distraction won't be conducive in firing up your creative flow.

Surround your working place with objects that makes you happy and relaxed. You may put up pictures, or scents, objects that inspire, or anything that can get your creativeness cranking. A clean and well organized workplace also rids of distractions and unwanted hindrances. With a good working place, you can work in peace and never notice the time pass by.

4) Set the mood.

Setting the mood requires you to just go with the moment or to induce your self to feeling what makes your mind works best. Finding out what makes you tick could help you find ways to get your creative juices flowing. Set the pace and tempo for your mood and everything else will follow.

There are many ways to set the mood. Some writers have been known to use alcohol, a little sip of wine to stir up the imagination.

Some would like some mood music while others let the lighting of the environment create the mood.

5) Go on a getaway and just do something unlike crazy.

Letting yourself go and have fun produces adrenaline that can make your imagination go wild. Take an adventure or a solemn hike. Whatever it is that is unusual from your daily routine can take the rut out of your schedule. In no time at all, your creativeness will make use of that experience and get your imagination to go on overdrive.

WHAT TO DO BEFORE SUBMITTING TO ARTICLE DIRECTORIES

To all writers and non-writers out there, now is the time to start digging up those creative writing skills back.

With modern communication technology comes the popularity of information-based marketing, which is one of the oldest and most effective techniques in getting targeted prospects to sites and converting them into buyers. This is why article writing, submissions and publications are also getting popular.

There are already many tools that people can use to make the process of distributing their articles more easily. Though this is invaluable in getting the contents more exposure, which is only half of the story. Let us take a look first at the common mistakes that some people make before submitting their contents to article directories:

1. Confusing the reason to promote the articles with the reason to write them.

In article writing, there are three key benefits why you are promoting them; branding, lead generation and promotion, which are all part of your optimization efforts.

But there is only one reason why you write an article, and that is to inform your audience. If the article is not focused on this primary and most important purpose, it will fail to achieve the three promotion benefits because no one will be interested in reading them.

You need to figure out first how to get people to read what is in your article, then make them click on your resource box. You can achieve this by producing better contents.

2. Failing to maximize the promotional opportunities of article marketing.

You may know already that your articles can help you generate additional links back to your site.

But do you know that you can get more visitors and better search engine results from that same articles?

Mention keywords at strategic places. Just be sure not to overdo them. Some are even using anchor texts which is also an effective method. But it is important to know that majority of the directories are not able to support this.

Remember that is not only about the links back to your site. Part of doing well in your article marketing is getting picked up by publishers with a large number of audiences and gaining the ability of leveraging other brands because of the quality of your work. Better search engine results also are great benefits.

But these things do not put much money in your pocket. There are other factors that can turn your article marketing efforts into an opportunity that can boost your earnings. Not just increase the number of visitors to your site.

Start out with a plan and see to it that your article will serve the function that you intended it to have.

3. Publishing content that does not help your readers.

Maybe in the process of writing articles, you are thinking that all that is you wanted is links back to your site. And any visitors it can generate are fine.
Guess what? Not all article banks and directories are going to accept your content automatically. Oftentimes, they have some guidelines and specifications on the articles that they are accepting.

You can double the number of sites you can submit to by writing articles that the directories want to share with other people. All it takes is one publisher with a hundred thousand readers to increase your potential audience overnight.

Write the articles that publishers want in their publications if you want your article marketing to work the most effective way for you. This also means you have to obey the standard guidelines, spell checks, researching on a good topic and even hiring a writer to produce a good content on your behalf.

In the end, it is all really a matter of choice on your part. You can start getting a little exposure from increased links back but on a very basic level. Or enjoy massive exposure from a little extra time making quality contents.

It will be your choice. You may not be aware of the fact that an article submitted on directories is not meant to have the same level of exposure as highly-targeted content ones geared on a narrow group of people.

Learn the difference between these two and it will surely help you know what kinds of articles to write and to submit.

RED HOT TIPS TO GET YOUR ARTICLES READ

There are many people who dread having to write papers or articles. Many just feel like it seems to be too much work and it all just goes to waste when no one reads the. To some people, reading articles seems like work to, especially if the article is boring and very bland. Well, articles are supposed to be read, that's their purpose to impart your message and information. If it is not read then it is a waste of time and effort.

But all the same, articles have to be written to be read. It's just a matter of making them good. Making a good article doesn't have to be strenuous and straining. There are just some points needed to be reminded of, and some guides to follow. Once you get the hang of it, writing articles could be fun, as well as profitable for you and your site.

Of course, writing articles must be about something you know about, that's why if you own a site, you probably is knowledgeable about that certain topic and theme.

When you write about it, you won't have a hard time because you already know what it is and what it's about. It's just a matter of making your articles creative and interesting.

To make sure that your articles get read and enjoyed, here are six red-hot tips to get your articles read. These tips will make your articles readable and interesting.

1) Use short paragraphs.

When the paragraph are very long, the words get jumbled in the mind of the reader just looking at it. It can get quite confusing and too much of a hard work to read. The reader will just quickly disregard the paragraph and move on to much easier reading articles that are good to look at as well as read. Paragraphs can be a single sentence, sometimes even a single word!

2) Make use of numbers or bullets.

As each point is stressed out, numbers and bullets can quickly make the point easy to remember and digest.

As each point, tip, guide or method is started with a bullet or point, readers will know that this is where the tips start and getting stressed. Format you bullets and numbers with indentations so that your article won't look like a single block of square paragraphs. Add a little bit of flair and pizzazz to your articles shape.

3) Use Sub-headings to sub-divide your paragraphs in the page.

Doing this will *break* each point into sections but still would be incorporated into one whole article. It would also be easy for the reader to move on from one point to another; the transition would be smooth and easy. You will never lose your readers attention as well as the point and direction to where the article is pointing.

4) Provide a good attention-grabbing title or header.

If your title can entice a person's curiosity you're already halfway in getting a person to read your article. Use statements and questions that utilize keywords that people are looking for.

Provide titles or headers that describe your articles content but should also be short and concise.

Use titles like, *"Tips on making her want you more"*, or *"How to make her swoon and blush"* .You could also use titles that can command people, for example, *"Make her yours in six easy Ways"*. These types of titles reach out to a persons' emotions and makes them interested.

5) Keep them interested from the start to the finish.

From your opening paragraph, use real life situations that can be adopted by the reader. Use good descriptions and metaphors to drive in your point, just don't over do it. Driving your examples with graphic metaphors and similes would make it easy for them to imagine what you are talking about. Making the experience pleasurable and enjoyable for them.

6) Utilize figures when necessary and not just ordinary and insipid statements.

Using specific facts and figures can heighten your article because it makes it authoritative.

But do not make it too formal, it should be light and easy in them and flow. Like a friendly teacher having a little chat with an eager student.

WRITING A RESOURCE BOX THAT MAKES PEOPLE CLICK

The Internet is the information highway, this phrase has been used so may time it should be nominated for the Internet Cliché Award. People that go to the Internet are subdivided into groups, but generally, they are out to search information. Whether for gaming, business, fun or anything else the Internet has provided us with information that has proved to be very beneficial.

Through the recent years many people have learned the secrets of Search Engine Optimization. More and more sites have seen the effects articles have done for the traffic of their sites.

Some have even created sites devoted entirely to providing articles that could be read by their website visitors and have links that could lead to many sites that are related to the topics and subjects of the articles.

For example, the sites may feature many articles about a whole lot of topics. As a website visitor reads the articles they have searched for, they can find at the end of the article a resource box that can be clicked on to link them to the site that has submitted the article. Of course the article would be in relation to the site. Lets say if the article is about rotating the tires, the resource box may lead to a link to a site that sells tires or car parts.

A resource box is what you usually find at the end of an article. They will contain the name of the author, a brief description of the author, a brief description of the sponsoring site and a link. If a reader likes what they read, they would have the tendency to find out where the article came from to read more. The resource bow will be their link to the source of the article and this will entice them to go to the site and do some more reading or research for the subject or topic they are interested in.

But like the article itself, the resource box must also be **eye-catching** to demand the attention and interest of the reader. While the resource bow encompasses only a small space, providing the right keywords and content for your resource box will provide more prodding for the reader to go to your site.

Now we know what resource boxes are, what are the benefits of having a good resource box?

Mainly its driving traffic to your site.

Many sites would allow articles to be placed in their sites because they can make use of the articles to fill their pages. They also get affiliation with other sites that can be beneficial for them as well. For the sponsoring site, when you get people to click on your resource box, you generate traffic that can be counted upon as potential customers.

So what would be a good content for your resource box? Basically it is keywords, learning about the proper keywords that people are mainly searching for. There are many tools you can find in the Internet that can help you in determining what keywords to use.

Resource boxes can also make use of all the creativity it can get. You only get a small space for your resource box so you better make the most of it. Try to catch the attention of your reader with resource box content that can make them give a second look. Unlike TV ads, you don't have visual aids to drive your point in.

But you do have the power of imagination of a reader. With the right content, you can make them think and intrigued.

Another tip is to use keywords that should be related to your site. Do not mislead your potential website visitors. Build your credibility so that more people would get enticed to visit your site and browse what you have to offer. Make the people click your resource box by providing resource box content that makes a lasting impression. You only get one chance to wow them and hundreds of chances to repulse them.

Never underestimate the power of the resource box. It may be small in size but they will provide a significant aid in driving traffic to your site. A boring resource box will never get a job done. Be fun and creative but at the same time show that you have a great deal to offer, too much to ask for something that couldn't fit a paragraph? Yes and no, there are many tips and guides that can help you in doing this, the first step is realizing how important a resource box could be in making people click your link and be directed to your site.

IF YOU HATE WRITING ARTICLES...

Owning, running and maintaining an Internet based business or a site needs articles. Plain and simple, every one who has a site knows this. Even those who don't have sites but are frequent Internet users knows this as well. Articles quench the thirst for information and knowledge of the people. Plus, the articles provide many other benefits for the site.

The benefits that articles provide are putting a site high in the ranking in search results of keywords and keyword phrases that pertains or are relevant to his or her site. They also provide attraction to website visitors when they are appreciated and is linked to your site from another site or newsletter. Articles provide for the increase of the confidence and trust levels of customers to your site and company.

Many articles are also beneficial to both company and its traffic.

When the readers like the articles, they would tell more of their friends, family and peers and recommend your site to them, providing for a larger volume of traffic. You get bigger sales if your traffic trusts and believes in you. Your product or services would be much easier to sell when they know you know what you are doing and talking about.

So ok, we have established that articles are very important to a site and to business. Articles are crucial and to keep ahead in the game, a site must have an article, it is imperative. There is one dilemma though, not many people like writing articles.

Many website owners would rather spend their time on something else, and unless you're a big time company, you don't have the necessary resources to use on a pool of article writers. Plagiarism or copying of other articles is frowned upon and could easily get you into trouble, worst case scenario; a hefty fine and jail time.

So what are the other options?

Well, for starters if you hate writing articles and you can't afford to hire people to write for you then don't.

Get free articles. The first place to look at for free articles is the public domain. Here you won't have problems with copyright infringement and the following penalties and fines if you get caught for plagiarism.

Public domain articles are articles freely given to the public for public use. You can do whatever you want with it. You can place it on your site, name it as yours, put it in a newsletter its you decision. Always remember though that you will have to choose articles that is very relevant to your site.

The downside to public domain articles is that since it is free for everybody, many of your competitors may have access to them as well. Since every site needs to be original and unique even though you have the same niche, this could be a predicament. You may also have to edit them a bit to place more keywords and keyword phrases to make them better.

Another way to get free articles is to **allow other sites which has the same subject or topic as yours to submit articles to your site.**

This would be only to augment your existing content or else all your articles would be leading to other sites since these articles would have resource boxes with them that could link or direct the readers to their site. That's why it is important to have your own articles; you cold use them to link your site to other sites as well.

Tip: to truly feel the impact of what a good article to you, go for original ones. There are many article writers who do part time and freelance article writing jobs that charges only minimal fees. You can get good articles that have all the keywords and keyword phrases you need and people are looking for.

The investment you made for these articles would be worthwhile because you could use them for all the benefits you could offer. You hold copyrights to them and you will be able to use them anyway you want.

As your articles help you in building your business and your site, you will have more articles to write and maybe then you wont be having second thoughts about articles.

7

CHARLES DARWIN

Chiloé

Edición bilingüe (bilingual edition) por (by) David Yudilevich

EDITORIAL UNIVERSITARIA

IMAGEN DE CHILE